SUNDAY SOLOS
IN THE KEY OF C

ISBN 978-1-5400-6358-8

Visit Hal Leonard Online at
www.halleonard.com

Contact us:
Hal Leonard
7777 West Bluemound Road
Milwaukee, WI 53213
Email: info@halleonard.com

In Europe, contact:
Hal Leonard Europe Limited
42 Wigmore Street
Marylebone, London, W1U 2RN
Email: info@halleonardeurope.com

In Australia, contact:
Hal Leonard Australia Pty. Ltd.
4 Lentara Court
Cheltenham, Victoria, 3192 Australia
Email: info@halleonard.com.au

ABOVE ALL

Words and Music by PAUL BALOCHE
and LENNY LeBLANC

ANCIENT OF DAYS

Words and Music by GARY SADLER
and JAMIE HARVILL

Steady drive

EL SHADDAI

Words and Music by MICHAEL CARD
and JOHN THOMPSON

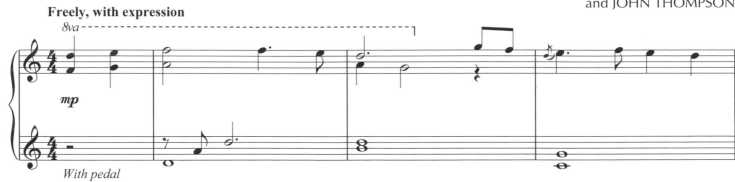

GOOD GOOD FATHER

Words and Music by PAT BARRETT
and ANTHONY BROWN

To Coda ⊕

rall.

FROM THE INSIDE OUT

Words and Music by
JOEL HOUSTON

HIS NAME IS WONDERFUL

Words and Music by
AUDREY MIEIR

With movement

GREAT IS THE LORD

Words and Music by MICHAEL W. SMITH
and DEBORAH D. SMITH

Broadly, not too fast

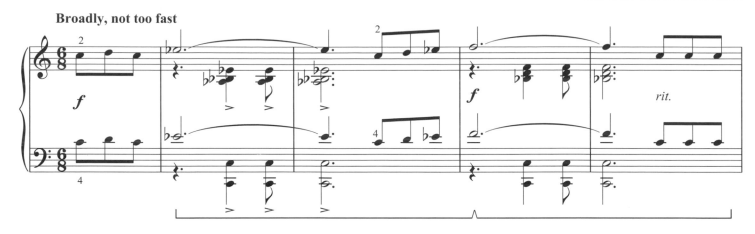

With hushed intensity

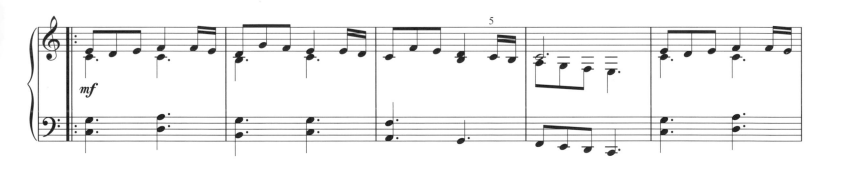

HOLY SPIRIT

Words and Music by KATIE TORWALT
and BRYAN TORWALT

Worship Ballad

With pedal

Bring out melody

HOW HE LOVES

Words and Music by
JOHN MARK McMILLAN

Slowly, in 2

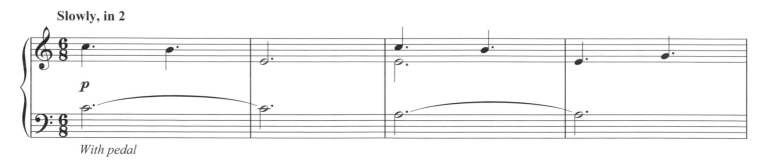

With pedal

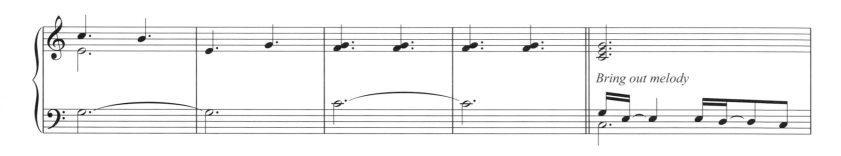

Bring out melody

KING OF MY HEART

Words and Music by JOHN MARK McMILLAN
and SARAH McMILLAN

31

JESUS MESSIAH

Words and Music by CHRIS TOMLIN,
JESSE REEVES, DANIEL CARSON
and ED CASH

With praise

LORD, I NEED YOU

Words and Music by JESSE REEVES,
KRISTIAN STANFILL, MATT MAHER,
CHRISTY NOCKELS and DANIEL CARSON

NONE BUT JESUS

Words and Music by
BROOKE LIGERTWOOD

OUR GOD

Words and Music by JONAS MYRIN,
JESSE REEVES, CHRIS TOMLIN
and MATT REDMAN

OCEANS
(Where Feet May Fail)

Words and Music by JOEL HOUSTON,
MATT CROCKER and SALOMON LIGHTHELM

Moderately slow

RECKLESS LOVE

Words and Music by CALEB CULVER,
CORY ASBURY and RAN JACKSON

Slowly, in 2

To Coda ⊕

D.S. al Coda

SWEET, SWEET SPIRIT

Words and Music by
DORIS AKERS

WE ARE AN OFFERING

Words and Music by
DWIGHT LILES

WHAT A BEAUTIFUL NAME

Words and Music by BEN FIELDING
and BROOKE LIGERTWOOD

With freedom

Moderately, in tempo

WHOM SHALL I FEAR
(God of Angel Armies)

Words and Music by CHRIS TOMLIN,
ED CASH and SCOTT CASH

WORD OF GOD SPEAK

Words and Music by BART MILLARD
and PETE KIPLEY

Prayerfully, with reverence

YOU ARE MY ALL IN ALL

By DENNIS JERNIGAN

Light Classical feel